Mel Bay presents

Italian Songs

& Arias for Accordion

by Gary Dahl

1 2 3 4 5 6 7 8 9 0

Visit us on the Web at www.melbay.com — E-mail us at email@melbay.com

CONTENTS

INTRODUCTION

Welcome to the world of beautiful Italian music. This is a book that contains many of the beloved arias and traditional favorites that pour out the deepest of emotions. Some of the world's greatest composers and singers have expressed themselves in this sublime musical language. Many of the pieces in this book have never been arranged for today's modern accordion utilizing all of its superb orchestral capabilities.

Ciao,

Gary Dahl

FOREWORD

Joe Spano was truly one of the greatest teachers of accordion. Students of Joe Spano have won world competition titles and many national titles, and, most importantly, hundreds of his former students still play professionally and for personal enjoyment. Gary Dahl studied with Joe Spano and today continues his productive teaching philosophy.

About this book: This book contains many arias as well as traditional favorites that have never been arranged for accordion utilizing all of its superb orchestral capabilities including arias such as Nessun Dorma, Quando Men Vo, and O Mio Babbino Caro to name a few.

This book is dedicated to the memory of Joe Spano 1920-1992

TELEPHONE POLKA

Traditional
Dedicated to Al Monti, Myron Floren and Toby Hanson

Arr. by Gary Dahl

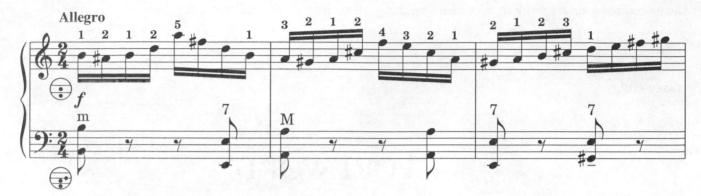

Use third finger on repeat.

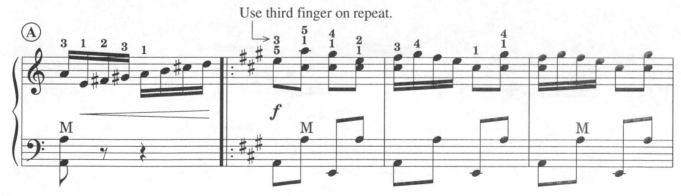

ITALIA

Dedicated to the memory of Joe Spano (1920 - 1992)

Gary Dahl
1998

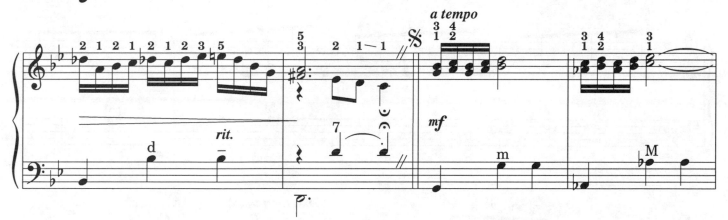

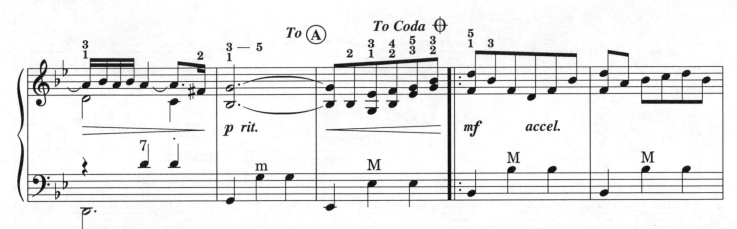

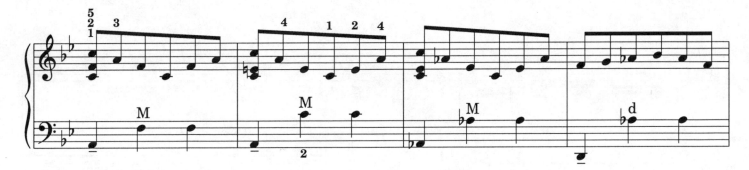

Largo

D.S. % al Coda ⊕

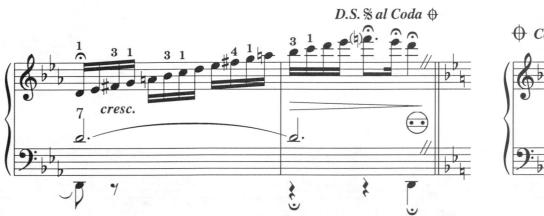

⊕ Coda

cresc.

rit.

molto largo

molto espress. e cresc.

the final hours

f > p

morendo

pp

NESSUN DORMA

Turandot
Dedicated to the memory of Guro Kristine Klokk

Puccini
Arr. by Gary Dahl

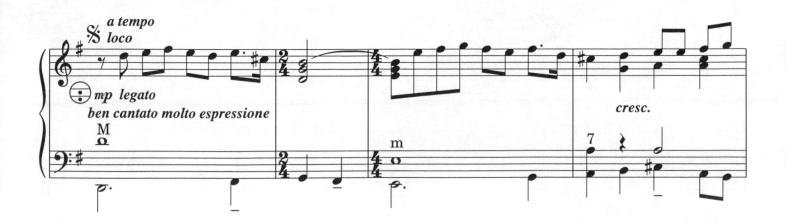

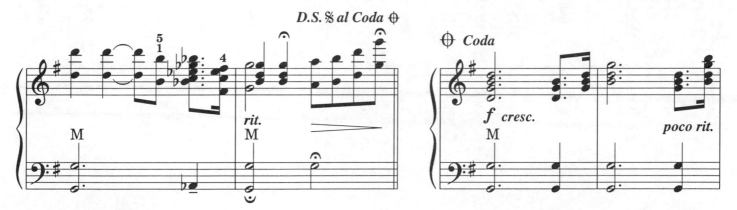

O MIO BABBINO CARO

Gianni Schicchi
This arrangement is dedicated to the memory of Joe Spano

Orchestral Version

Puccini
Arr. by Gary Dahl

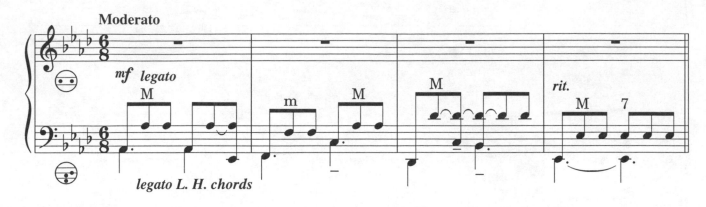

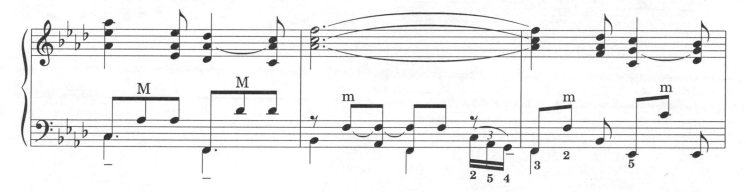

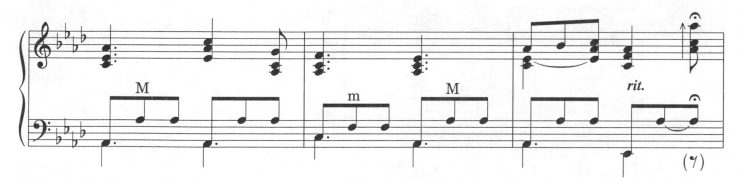

QUANDO MEN VO

from
La Bohème

This arrangement is dedicated to my daughter Leesa; Concert Pianist

Puccini
Arr. by Gary Dahl

Musetta: Con molta grazia ed eleganza

14

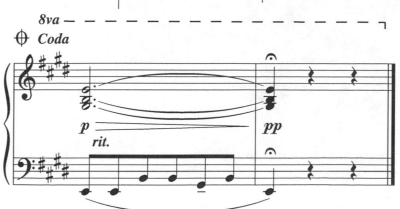

MATTINATA

Morning Serenade
Dedicated to the memory of Mel Bay

Ruggiero Leoncavallo
Arr. by Gary Dahl

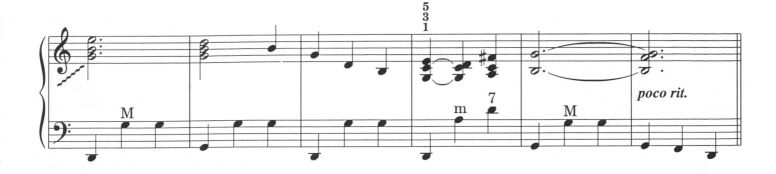

UNA FURTIVA LAGRIMA

A Furtive Tear
L'elisir d'amore

Donizetti
Arr. by Gary Dahl

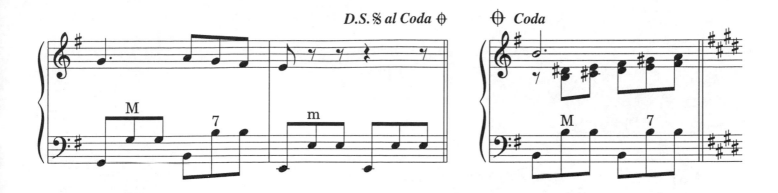

19

M'APPARI TUTT 'AMOR

She Seemed to Me
Martha

Von Flotow
Arr. by Gary Dahl

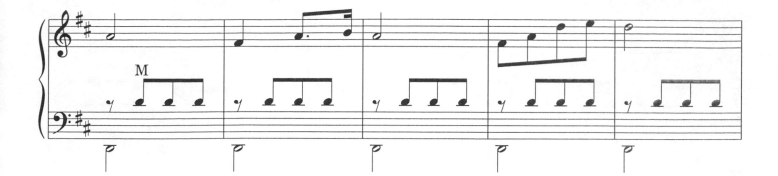

a tempo

L. H. non legato

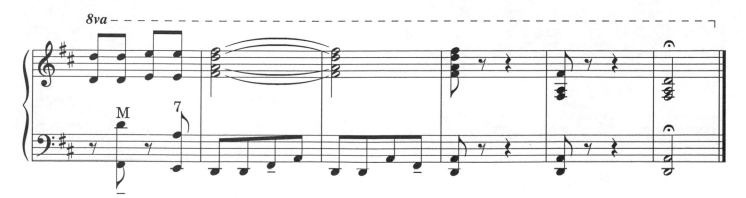

UN BEL DI VEDREMO

(One Fine Day)

Madama Butterfly

This arrangement is dedicated to my wife Eloise

Puccini
Arr. by Gary Dahl

This page has been left blank to avoid awkward page turns.

COME BACK TO SORRENTO

Single Note Version

Ernesto de Curtis
Arr. by Gary Dahl

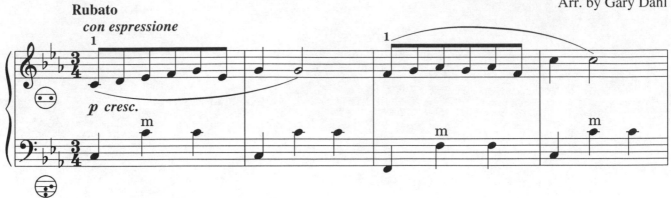

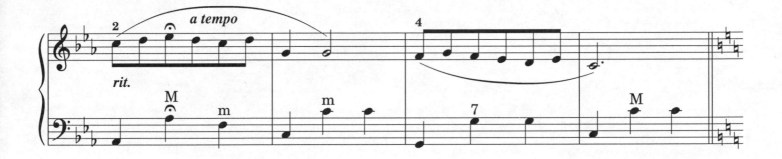

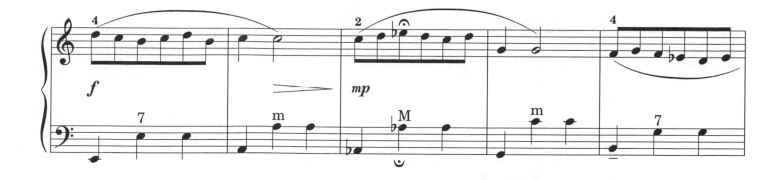

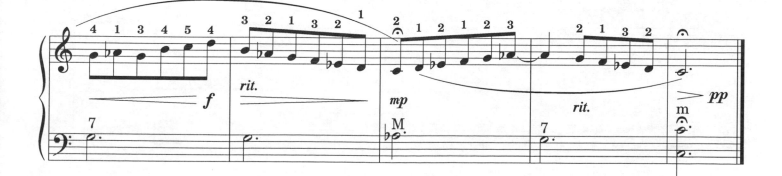

COME BACK TO SORRENTO

Dedicated to Joe Petosa Sr.
petosa accordions

Advanced

Ernesto de Curtis
Arr. by Gary Dahl

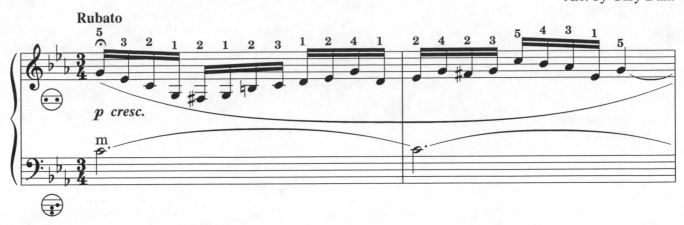

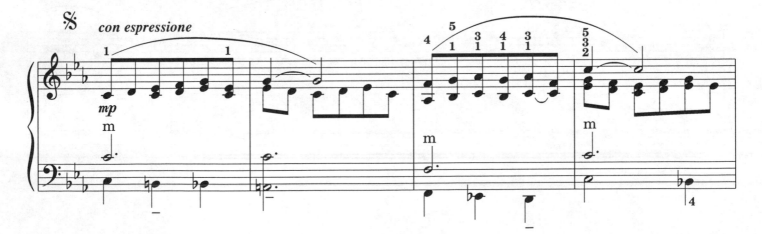

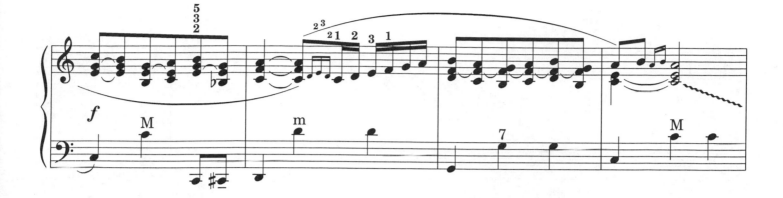

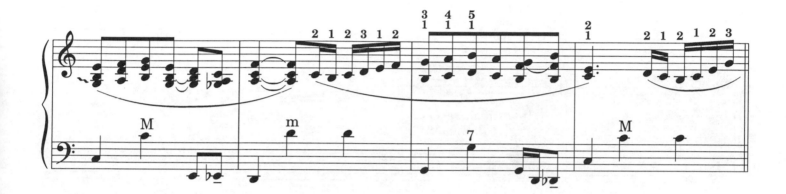

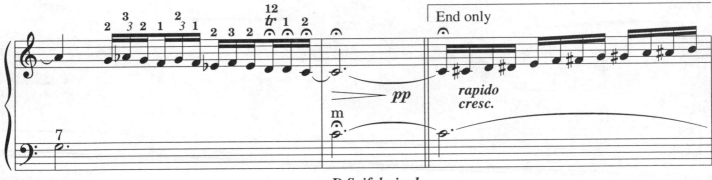

D.S. if desired
with ⊕ and 8va

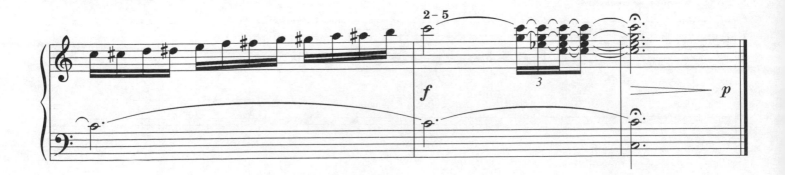

LIBIAMO RE' LIETI CALICI

Drinking - Song
La Traviata
Dedicated to my father, Joe Dahl

Verdi
Arr. by Gary Dahl

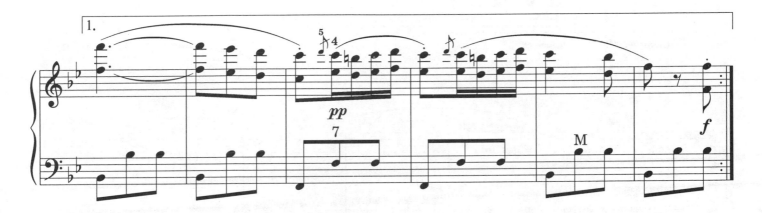

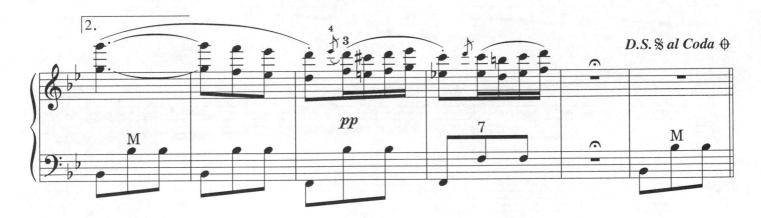

First time low B♭ only, both notes on repeat.

trem B♭, Hold F and D

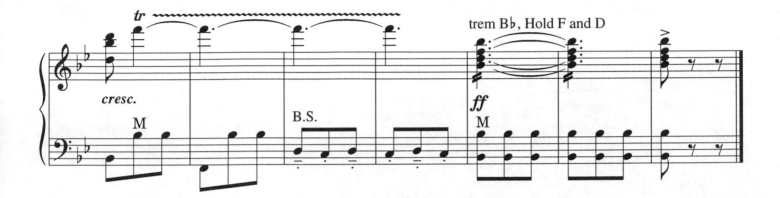

LA TRAVIATA

Prelude
Dedicated to Ron Ostromecki

Verdi
Arr. by Gary Dahl

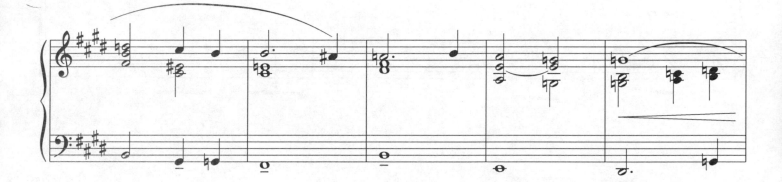

O MIO BABBINO CARO

Gianni Schicchi

This arrangement is dedicated to the memory of Joe Spano

Single Note Version

Puccini
Arr. by Gary Dahl

This page has been left blank to avoid awkward page turns.

LA DONNA E MOBILE

Verdi
Arr. by Gary Dahl

To Coda ⊕   D.S. al Coda ⊕   ⊕

MARIANNA

Italian Folk Song

Arr. by Gary Dahl

Allegretto

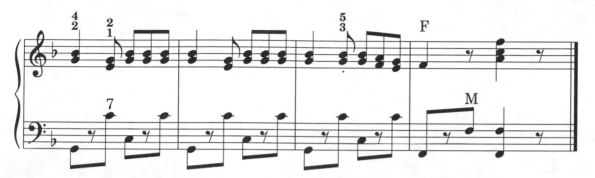

TARANTELLA NAPOLETANA

Dedicated to Bruce Metras
The Italian Stallion

By L. Crisculo
Arr. by Gary Dahl

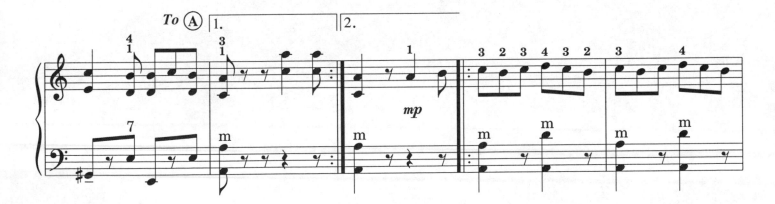

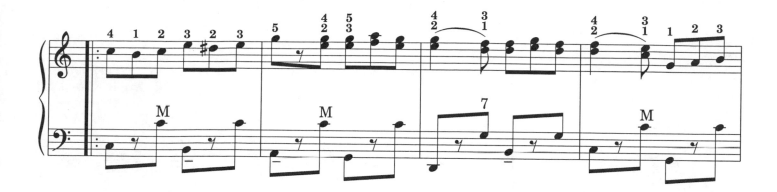

VICINO LA MARE

Traditional
Arr. by Gary Dahl

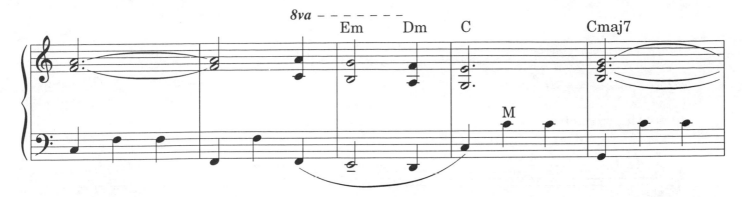

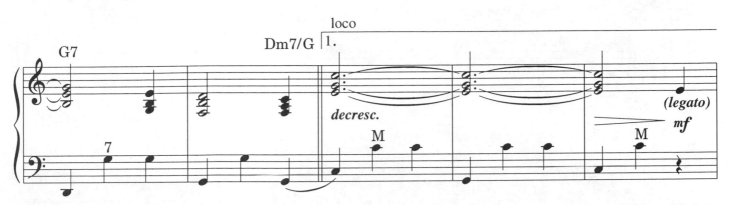

LA DANZA

Dedicated to John Castiglione
Castiglione Accordion and Distributing Co.

G. Rossini
Arr. by Gary Dahl

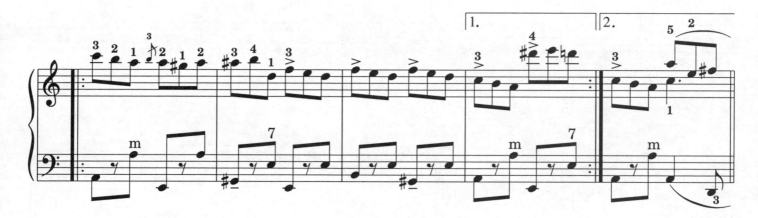

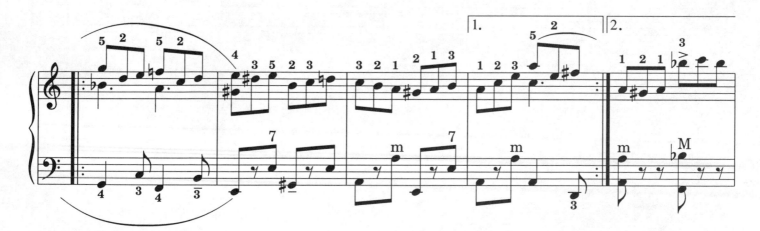

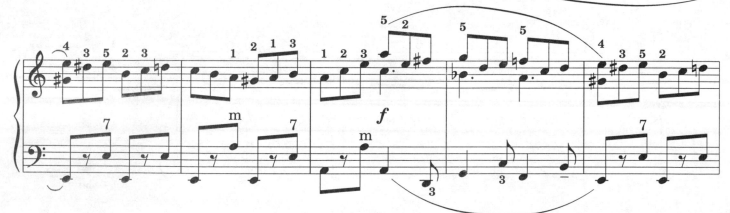

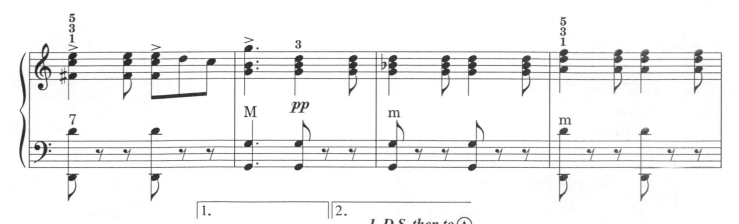

1. D.S. then to Ⓐ
2. D.S. al ⊕

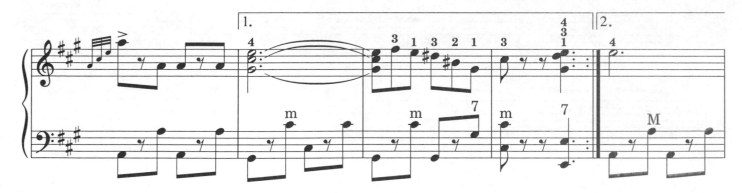

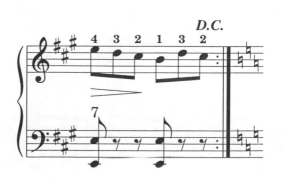

⊕ **Coda**
8va

'O MARENARIELLO

The Sailor

S. Gambardella
Arr. by Gary Dahl

55

SEBBEN CRUDELE

(Savage and Heartless is Your Cruel Scorn)
Aria from Opera Pastorale

Antonio Caldara
1670-1736
Arr. by Gary Dahl

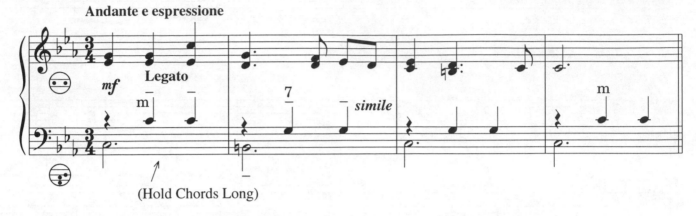

(Hold Chords Long)

D.S. 𝄋 (*1st time only*)

D.S.𝄋al Coda ⨁   ⨁ *Coda*

molto rit.

LA SPAGNOLA

The Spanish Girl

Vicenzo d. Chiara
Arr. by Gary Dahl

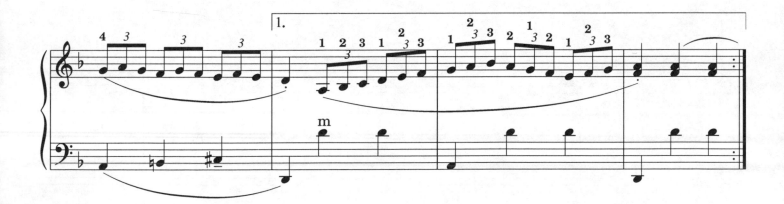

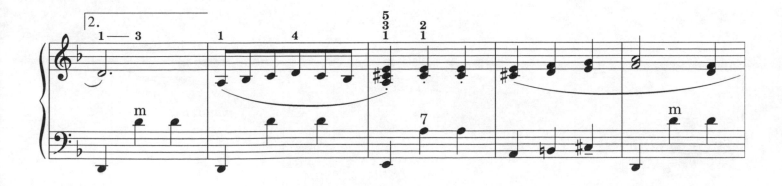

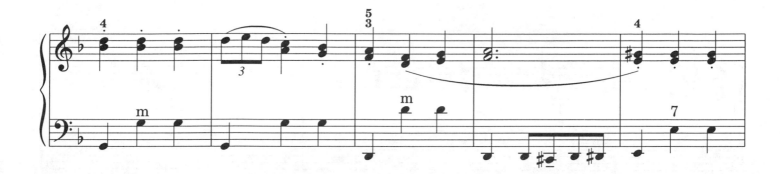

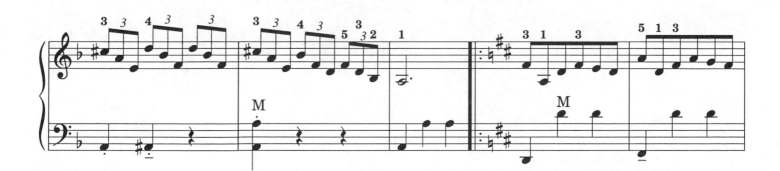

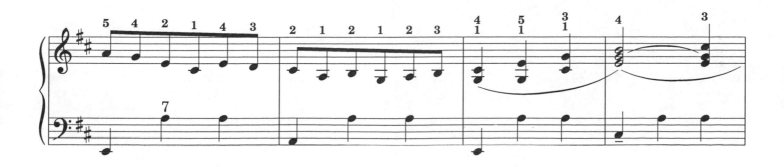

This page has been left blank to avoid awkward page turns.

SANTA LUCIA

Valse Andantino

Arr. by Gary Dahl

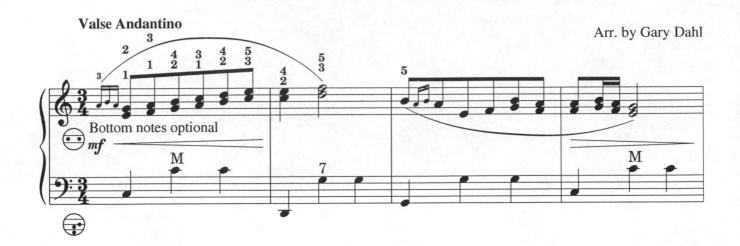

Bottom notes optional

To Coda

1.   2.   *D.C. al Coda* ⊕   ⊕ *Coda*

VIENI SUL MAR

Oh, Come to the Sea

Neapolitan Song
Arr. by Gary Dahl

Tempo di valse

ANVIL CHORUS

from Il Trovatore

Verdi
Arr. by Gary Dahl

Allegro

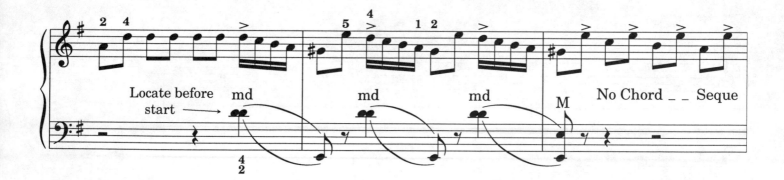

Moderato

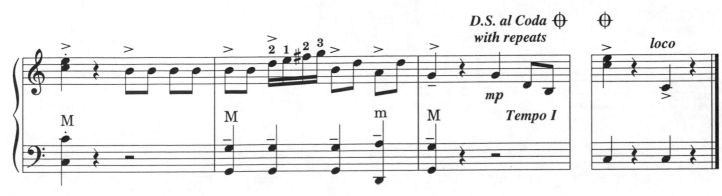

* Tenuto: Sustained; or Full Value

O SOLE MIO

Dedicated to Tom Demski, Mr. Flash!

E. Di Capua
Arr. by Gary Dahl

Andantino con espressione

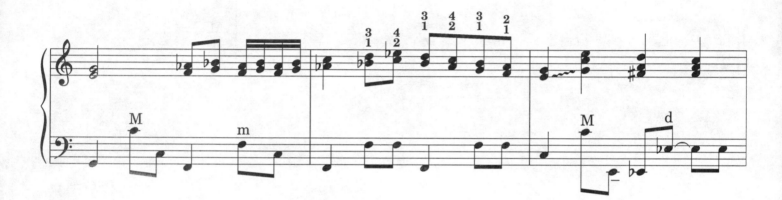

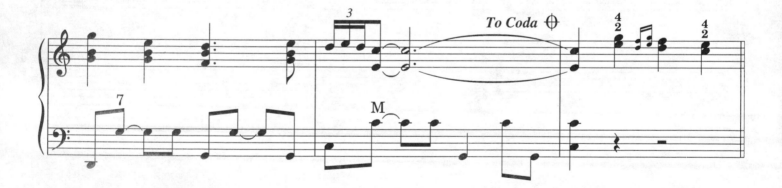

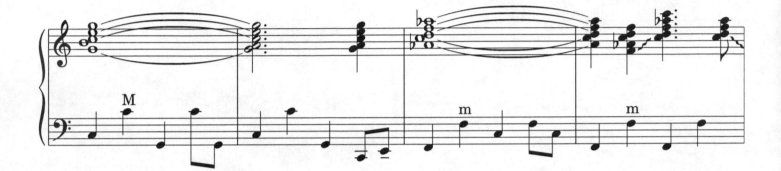

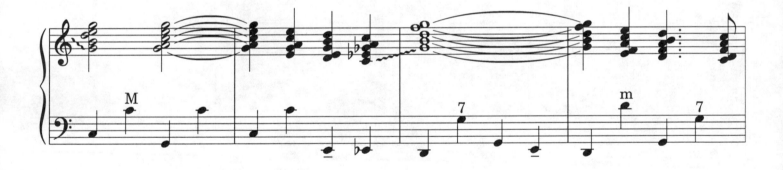

70

This page has been left blank to avoid awkward page turns.

A SERENATA DE ROSE

The Serenade of the Rose
Dedicated to my mother Adeline

Edvardo di Capua
Arr. by Gary Dahl

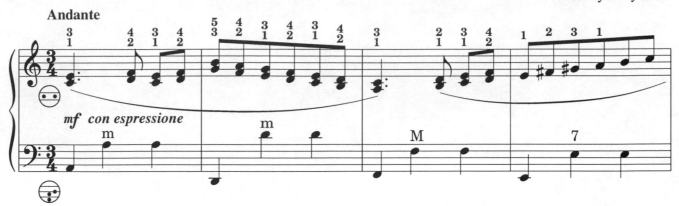

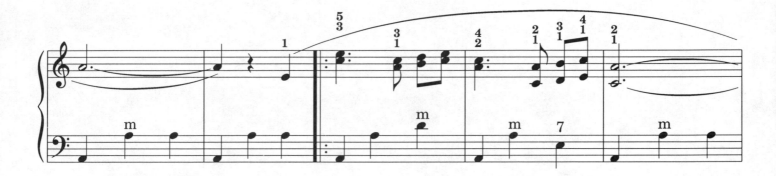

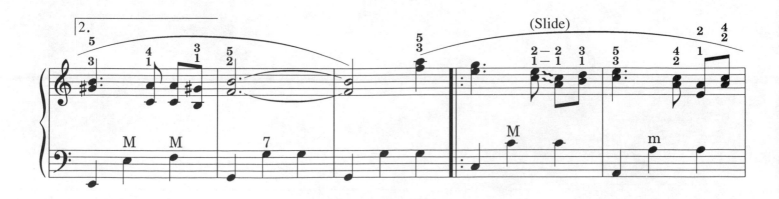

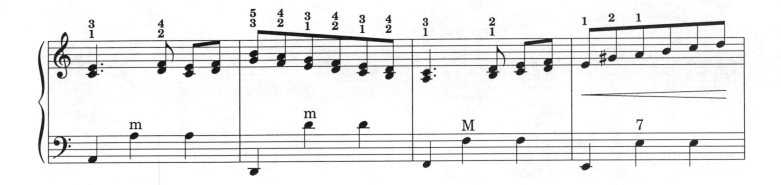

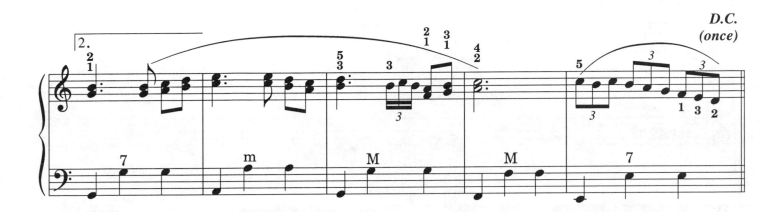

rit. poco a poco decresc. poco a poco

MARIA MARI

E. Dicapua
Arr. by Gary Dahl

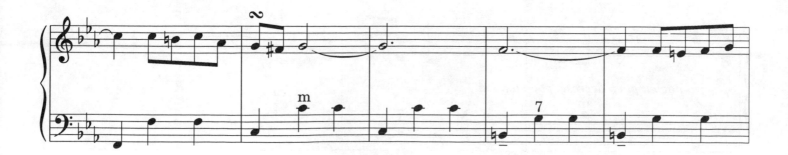

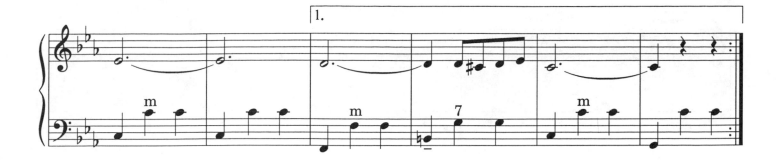

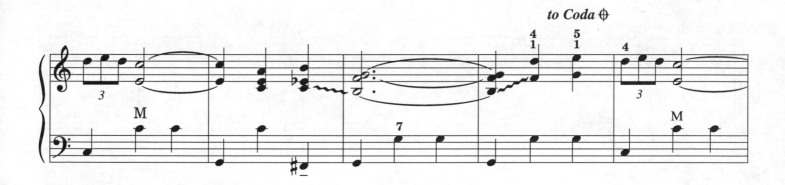

to Coda ⊕

D.S. al Coda ⊕   ⊕

About the Author

Gary Dahl, a former commercial pilot and corporate regional sales manager is currently active as an accordionist, composer, arranger, recording artist and educator residing in Puyallup (close to Seattle) Washington. He received a BA degree from the University of Washington with a minor in music theory, composition and harmony. Mr. Dahl's students have been consistent winners in national and state competitions and many have achieved professional status. The Gary Dahl Trio has performed regularly at private clubs, hotels and the lounge circuit. (1960 - 1991) Gary currently performs as a single for exclusive private venues. A recognized teacher, Gary Dahl provides specialized training for all levels of students including lessons by correspondence through the Gary Dahl Accordion School. Please visit: www.accordions.com/garydahl.